12/10

D1560437

DATE DUE

JUN 25 2012		
OCLC 7/9/13		
ISSAQUAH WA		
OCLC 8/7/13		
Waukegan IL		
OCLC 9/28/13		
Warrensburg MO		

Demco, Inc. 38-293

THE BEGGAR'S
Blessing
Based on a true story

Retold by Mark Hamby

ILLUSTRATED BY DEBORAH AND JENNIFER HAMBY

II Samuel 24:24

LAMPLIGHTER
PUBLISHING

Waverly, Pennsylvania
Copyright © September, 2000, 2002, May, 2005, May 2009 by Mark Hamby
ISBN-10:1-58474-052-3 ISBN-13:978-1-58474-052-0

1-888-246-7735
www.lamplighterpublishing.com

 ong ago in a quiet English village, the merry tune of the woodcarver brightened each morning as he opened his shop. The carver was a skillful worker who turned rough wood into beautiful furniture, dolls, and toys.

He was delighted when children visited his shop, especially as they marveled at his new creations.

here was one child of whom the carver was particularly fond. Her name was Katura. Once a week Katura made her way to the woodcarver's shop and spent her time gazing at the wonderful carvings, especially the doll in the velvet green dress.

 he doll was so lovely, with her glassy blue eyes, soft silky hair, and delicate face. Katura was determined that some day the doll would be hers.

Katura worked hard, and month after month she saved her shillings.

inally, the long awaited day came. She placed her shillings in her leather pouch and tightly tied the strings.

Never had there been a happier child. Filled with anticipation, Katura hastily made her way to the village.

s she merrily skipped along the path, Katura's heart leaped with joy as she caught a glimpse of the wood-carver's shop.

xcitedly, yet with humble dignity she entered the wood-carver's shop, pointed to the doll of her desire, handed the woodcarver his due and joyfully received her long awaited treasure. Now, with the precious doll in her arms, the little lady bade the woodcarver good afternoon as she began her stroll back home.

 s Katura stepped on to the cobblestone street, a poor miserable looking object of a man met her eye.

He was standing but a few steps away and seemed as though he were going to speak to her.

ttracted, doubtless by the innocent kindliness of her expression and the tenderness of her blue eyes, his lips moved, but no sound came from them.

He stood aside to let her pass, with a mute agonized appeal in his sunken cheeks and quivering chin.

"Did you wish to speak to me?" asked the little lady, staying her steps.

ncouraged by her winsome voice, the poor man said in trembling accents, "I am very hungry. I would not ask for help if I were not ready to sink with hunger," he pleaded with famined eyes and outstretched arms.

 am so sorry. I have no money, nor food, or I would surely help thee."

His lips whispered forth a humble, "Thank you my lady," as he shuffled on his way, hunger impersonate.

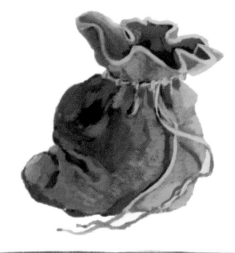

tay!" cried the little owner of the new doll.

There was a quiver in her childish voice and moisture in her blue eyes as she softly spoke. "Please, wait."

The beggar turned slowly and rested his weary body as he beheld Katura fondly gazing upon her precious doll.

ithin moments Katura knew what she had to do. With a determined gait she walked back into the woodcarver's shop. "Please sir, may I exchange my doll for the shillings that I paid for her?" "Are you not satisfied with your new doll, my child?" "Oh yes, sir, but there is someone who needs these shillings more than I need this lovely doll."

arrying her coin-filled pouch, Katura hurried out of the shop, smiled, and placed the whole of her savings into the hands of the starving man.

He was like one thunderstruck! Never before had bounty reigned upon him in such profusion.

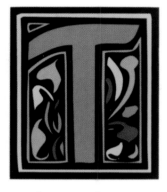he object of her
mercy murmured in
a low tone, though
loud enough to reach her ear. "If
the Almighty made you a queen, it
would not be more than your
goodness deserves."

As the little girl embraced the
beggar with a compassionate
gesture of affection, he
whispered, "Indeed, my child, may
the Almighty God some day make
you a queen."

 everal years later,
Katura became
England's youngest
girl ever to be crowned.
Her name - Queen Victoria.

And so it is as Jesus said, "When you have done it unto the least of these, my brethren, you have done it unto me."

Matthew 25:40

For I was hungry and you gave Me food; I was thirsty and you gave Me drink; I was a stranger and you took Me in; I was naked and you clothed Me; I was sick and you visited Me; I was in prison and you came to Me.